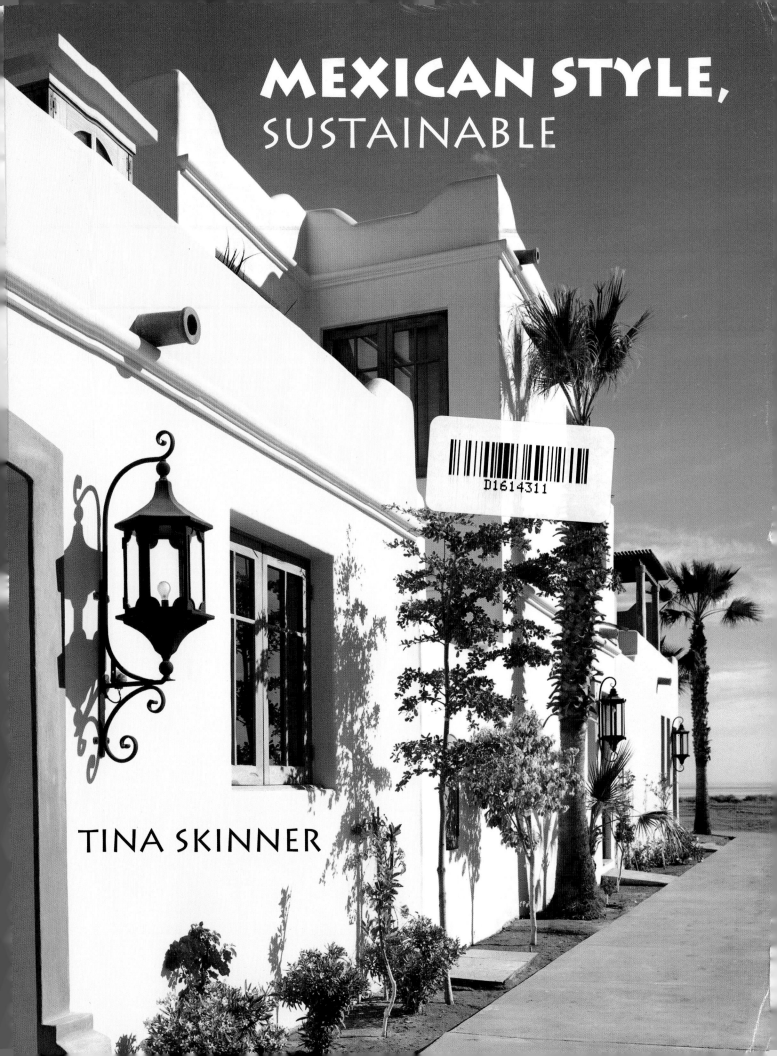

MEXICAN STYLE,
SUSTAINABLE

TINA SKINNER

Designed by John P. Cheek
Cover design by Bruce Waters
Type set in Caslon 224 BK BT/Humanist 521 BT

ISBN: 978-0-7643-2743-8
Printed in China

Published by Schiffer Publishing Ltd.
4880 Lower Valley Road
Atglen, PA 19310
Phone: (610) 593-1777; Fax: (610) 593-2002
E-mail: Info@schifferbooks.com

For the largest selection of fine reference books on this and related subjects, please visit our web site at
www.schifferbooks.com
We are always looking for people to write books on new and related subjects. If you have an idea for a book please contact us at the above address.

This book may be purchased from the publisher.
Include $3.95 for shipping.
Please try your bookstore first.
You may write for a free catalog.

In Europe, Schiffer books are distributed by
Bushwood Books
6 Marksbury Ave.
Kew Gardens
Surrey TW9 4JF England
Phone: 44 (0) 20 8392-8585; Fax: 44 (0) 20 8392-9876
E-mail: info@bushwoodbooks.co.uk
Website: www.bushwoodbooks.co.uk
Free postage in the U.K., Europe; air mail at cost.

Contents

Acknowledgments

To Laura Mikowychok, intern extraordinaire. To Caitlin Falzone, who kept this project in motion when it threatened to stall. And to all the folks at Loreto Bay who give "development" a good name.

Introduction

Mexican legend says that Loreto, Mexico is "the place where the mountains come to swim." This may be true, as the line of Sierra de la Giganta mountains gradually disappear into the waters of Loreto Bay, but these days more than the mountains are jumping in.

When a couple looking for a place to retire stumbled upon this Mexican paradise, they knew crystal waters and abundant wildlife made Loreto Bay the perfect spot to build an entire community. But instead of bulldozing the palm trees and paving the shore to erect tall hotels and beach resorts, they insisted upon leaving Loreto Bay in better shape than it was when they arrived. With the help of the Loreto Bay Foundation and Loreto Bay Company, a sustainable community is growing on this Baja shore, giving back to its environment, improving quality of life, and providing economic opportunities.

Construction has begun; stunning Mexican-inspired architecture and city grids inspired by New Urbanism now grace the seaside town, while vast wildlife preserves reach into the mainland and offer protected space to hundreds of native species. Inside the growing development of Loreto, dusty streets suddenly lead into pristine developments, where marvelous adobe homes sit surrounded by greenery,

View of the Loreto Bay Company's vision, from the sky.

with small plazas where neighbors might meet to gossip, and twisting sidewalks lead past gardens and mountain vistas.

In this book, we look at the questions Loreto Bay Company principals, Jim Grogan, Tom Nolan and David Butterfield, and their team continue to ask themselves as they seek to build their dream in The Villages of Loreto Bay.

An aerial view of the sustainable paradise that is Loreto Bay.

It Started with a Question

Imagine a place where every day the air is cleaner, the water is purer, the people are healthier, life is more abundant, and we are enriched by the culture.

We see ourselves on a journey, seeking to learn, working with partners, sharing our learning through dialogue, and growing the place we all imagine.

This is a story of imagination. Norma and David Butterfield started out with questions, and then shaped the answers from their dreams. Their question: If we could live in any kind of community, surrounded by any kind of landscape, living as part of any kind of neighborhood, what would it be like? David, president of the Trust for Sustainable Development, wanted to make those dreams come true. He was searching for a pace to retire.

Cliffs of the Sea of Cortez.

The Location: Loreto Bay

Norma and David wanted a warm, dry climate on the ocean, to build their dream. Southern California was too busy; they sought a close-knit community, but not a town as hectic as Los Cabos. While working on a project in La Paz, David happened across Loreto. Norma flew down that weekend.

What they'd "discovered" was a resort community that had faltered in its early stages of development by the Mexican government's tourism development board (FONATUR): A small airport, a hotel, a golf course, an unfinished convention center, a system of roads and sidewalks never fully realized, and the preservation of a mountain acquifer absorbed a huge investment, but the tourism payoff failed to materialize. Unlike Los Cabos at the southern tip of the peninsula, Loreto Bay failed to gain much notice. A relatively small economy was created by in-the-know fishermen, who flock to Loreto to enjoy what they describe as a tropical aquarium, teaming with fish, and liable to erupt at any moment with a sperm whale sighting.

South of the old city center of Loreto, the Mexican Government had at its command 8,000 acres overlooking the Sea of Cortez. In addition to sandy beaches, this included inland waterways, green arroyos, and arid mountains. The new master plan, as developed by the Butterfields, calls for approximately 6,000 homes for The Villages of Loreto Bay, with mixed-use buildings, narrow, walk-able streets and authentic Baja architecture that exists in harmony with its surroundings. Planned amenities include two eighteen-hole championship golf courses, a luxurious Beach Club and Spa, tranquil spas, a tennis center, a marina and sport fishing center, along with restaurants, boutiques, galleries, and a produce market.

Most importantly, though, the essence of Loreto Bay's utopian vision lies in a unique, progressive foundation: the Bay will be built as a sustainable community.

Loreto is a virtual paradise for fishermen, its water's teaming with sport fish, its weather almost always clement, and the promise of whale sightings an added allure. Boats, sea kayaks, and snorkel gear help fuel the local economy.

Visitors to the Villages of Loreto Bay are taken on nature hikes to explore the natural bio-diversity and rich resources of nearby arroyos.

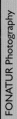

The expansive Loreto Bay Inn was developed by the Mexican government, and continues to welcome first-time guests to The Villages of Loreto Bay. Nearby, new properties invite them to return often, or retire here.

A sense of community is an important goal in the development plan for The Villages.

Streets lined with flowers and palm trees bring nature within the walls of a budding town, reminding urban residents they still live in a remote, organic paradise.

Werner Segarra Photography

Luxury spas with outdoor pools and enchanting lighting make this as much a tourist getaway as it is a prospering residential village.

The golf course, initially developed by FONATUR for the Loreto Bay resort, has suffered terribly in the desert-like conditions. A new agricultural research center is experimenting with turf that will thrive in the local conditions, while not polluting the area with chemicals or demanding too much water. Behind an experimental green, another patch of turf is being subjected to the rigorous test of avid football players: construction workers who enjoy their benefit of company sanctioned soccer.

Church bells call the faithful. The mission was the first on the Baja peninsula, and the ancient city still answers to its catholic roots.

Werner Segarra Photography

The Village developers work to form close ties between their development and the old city just to the north. Would-be homebuyers are introduced to the town, and its recommended restaurants. In this way they help fuel the local economy, and nurture a caring interdependence between old and new residents.

Dining at the Inn at Loreto Bay, where outdoor rooms attest to the area's mild climate, and lashed beams and posts.

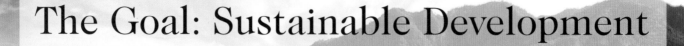

The Goal: Sustainable Development

Far from being a burden, sustainable development is an exceptional opportunity - economically, to build markets and create jobs; socially, to bring people in from the margins; and politically, to give every man and woman a voice, and a choice, in deciding their own future.

~UN Secretary-General Kofi Annan

Loreto Bay is the largest sustainable development under construction in North America today. But, what is sustainable development? The United Nations defines it as "meeting the needs of the present generation without sacrificing the ability of future generations to meet their own needs." Ask David Butterfield, Chair of Loreto Bay Company, and he'll tell you that it means following an "Intergenerational Golden Rule:" living so that our children can enjoy life as fully as we do. Of course, if you do get the chance to ask David about sustainability, be sure you've got time for a good, long talk. His knowledge is as thorough as his passion is contagious.

Then I say the earth belongs to each... generation during its course, fully and in its own right, no generation can contract debts greater than may be paid during the course of its own existence.

~Thomas Jefferson

Nursery stock in the development's agricultural research station will be used to green and beautify the growing village.

Photo by Russ Heinl

Early developers of the bay region thought it wise to drain the swamps and dredge navigable channels. The vision of the new, sustainable community is to develop cypress stands and restore the wetlands in the waterways surrounding the village. This will fuel and foster marine biodiversity in the region, and diversify the dinner offerings for fishermen. Since cypress are protected throughout Mexico, reintroducing them to the region is being done through the careful propagation of seeds and subsequent transplanting of hardy young trees.

The Vision

The Butterfields' first question shaped the vision for The Villages of Loreto Bay: The setting would be beautiful and inspiring. It would be set within an exotic, emerging country rich in history, authenticity, and vibrant culture. Yet, it would also provide all the comforts of home: clean water, excellent medical care, modern infrastructure, and safe streets. From the start, it would be planned for humans rather than for automobiles. Quiet, narrow streets would embrace residents, instead of noise and pollution, wide stretches of asphalt, and architecture dominated by garages. Walking to the Village Center, to the beach, or anywhere, would be a daily pleasure.

Photo by Russ Heinl

Adobe architecture in the warm tones associated with Mexico lend their authentic façades to a new Baja development.

Photo by Russ Heinl

Homes are given unique identities with coloring and detailing in woodwork and iron. The diversity makes the streetscape more interesting to explore. A dedication to developing landscaping suited to the environment makes it even more foot friendly.

Those who buy homes in the first phase of the Villages will probably subscribe to a beach culture, drawn to this place for its warm, clear waters, and brilliant sun. FONATUR assured that all the makings of a beach resort are in place, from cocktails by the sand, to thatched palapas and a well-groomed stretch for sunbathers.

The Architecture: How a City Grew

Walking these intimate organic pathways through the village is a sensual experience. Streets flow like streams; from wide to narrow, under archways, and in and out of sun-drenched courtyards. Fragrant bougainvillea vines trail over the tops of garden walls. Artisans show their hand in sculpted niches and benches in the rustic plastered walls. The very structure of this place and these planned opportunities for movement and stillness foster connections between people. [...] From simple human interaction the fabric of community is woven.

~Ayrie Cunliffe, Project Architect

Werner Segarra Photography

Rooftop porches make this city community unique. Most urban apartments seek to isolate residents from their many neighbors, but on a cool evening in Loreto Bay when many rise to their terraces, residents find an opportunity to connect and share the day's news.

A slatted trellis adds a layer of protection from a scorching sun midday, both for the home and for anyone who rises to enjoy the relief of cooling breezes that cross the low walls of the rooftops.

Photo by Russ Heinl

Werner Segarra Photography

Terracotta and teal blue capture the eye, in harmony with a desert landscape by the sea, overlooked by cactus-covered mountains.

A curvaceous penthouse crowns a private home, providing a room with a view.

Tonal shifts throughout the village both unify the homes and help establish their individuality.

Photo by Russ Heinl

Heat and steam are vented from the kitchen below through a slatted cupola, found on most of the homes in Loreto Bay.

Photo by Russ Heinl

Interconnectedness is stressed by proximity to neighbors. Access and association are enabled.

In the dream, a mix of housing types and prices will lead to a more diverse community of interesting people from all over the world. Human-scale architecture will be a wonderful expression of beauty and functionality. Landscaping appropriate to the habitat will be used to enhance the natural beauty of the surrounding wilderness. There is an Old World Mexican charm in the narrow, sinuous streets connecting to sunlight in courtyard after courtyard. Moving from shadow to splashes of light, refreshing fountains of water, vibrant colors, and the fragrance of bougainvillea, all the senses are invigorated.

The year-round temperate climate allows for indoor/outdoor living, making courtyard homes the most obvious design. Inspired by Spanish Colonial design, the architectural style ensures every home feels like a natural extension of the beautiful surroundings - desert, mountains and sea.

Every Loreto Bay home adheres to rigorous standards for sustainability. Built of natural local materials (earthen walls of locally mined and manufactured adobe blocks),

planned for energy and water conservation, and designed to protect and enhance the area's rich biodiversity, each home truly allows residents to live fully and tread lightly.

The Village Center will be an island located where it all flows together. Cafes, studios, and galleries will populate the edges of this vibrant Village Center and golfers will play through the center of the village like the best of Europe's old world courses. Plans call for performance spaces, gathering spaces, and wide promenades along the water's edge. Posadas, or small hotel apartments, will look down into the town square and out across the estuary to the sea and the Sierra de la Giganta mountains.

Finally, it would be a place where wellness-centered lives could thrive and learning would be a daily pursuit. A day of golf, fishing, kayaking, or whale-watching might end with a visit to a museum or gallery. Artistic, cultural, and intellectual pleasures would become a seamless part of the life of the community, and health and fitness would play a role in everyday living.

Photo by Russ Heinl

Wrought iron with motifs reminiscent of Aztec art trim the edges of most rooftop porches and outdoor staircases.

Photo by Russ Heinl

An exterior staircase within a home's central courtyard ascends to the second-floor rooms. In a climate where it only rains a few cumulative hours a year, there is no necessity to put a roof over everything.

Photo by Russ Heinl

Spiral staircases lead to third-story lofts with spectacular views.

Photo by Russ Heinl

A beautiful staircase climbs its way through winding walls to a rooftop terrace. Tiled risers and the sun-soaked tones of stucco contribute to this scene's Mexican character.

The proximity of the homes can actually aid in temperature control, keeping all but the hottest noontime sun off the narrow passageways.

Photo by Russ Heinl

Green oases are fostered in every available patch of land. There is also a push to add food-producing plant matter to streets and inner courtyards, helping to foster a garden culture that is self-sustaining.

Photo by Russ Heinl

A bird's-eye view affords a peek into a private garden, paved with stone and lovingly tended.

Climbing plants are quick to exploit the new development, bringing shade, color, and habitat into the new development.

Photo by Russ Heinl

Photo by Russ Heinl

This building boasts an organic façade, giving the structure the appearance of having grown in with the foliage. The goal of the village masterplan is to intermingle small business with residential areas, the opposite of a commuter community.

Photo by Russ Heinl

Werner Segarra Photography

With mountains to view, it is no accident that few buildings rise higher than the church steeples, the Mission, and a handful of high balconies with spiral staircases. Unobstructed by buildings, the scenery reaches all the way to street level, where benches, groves and courtyards invite residents to wander the quiet streets and enjoy the view, and each other.

It's all about levels in this seaside village, where multiple porch tiers on each home keep row after row of urban residents connected to the ocean by an unobstructed view. In addition to offering connections to each other, they also afford occupants the opportunity to get away by themselves. Half walls create an option of concealment or connect.

Photo by Russ Heinl

Photo by Russ Heinl

Sun worship is an ancient pursuit in Mexico, and a major lure for Gringos relocating south. New residents include a host of Canadians as well as Seattle and Oregon ex-pats in search of more rays.

A fearless use of traditional Mexican hues makes this a truly vibrant city.

Photo by Russ Heinl

Every inch of a Loreto Bay home has been lovingly designed. Here a staircase embellished with Mexican tile ascends to a signature rooftop porch.

Maximizing sustainability, homes in Loreto Bay give back to their residents with energy efficiency and natural material construction. Clay roof tiles and drain spouts continue a tradition first brought to the region by Spanish missionaries in the late 1600s.

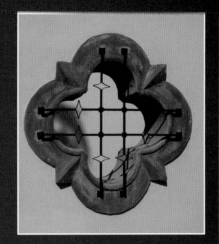

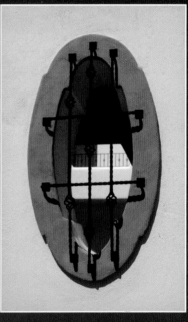

Window details in keeping with Mexican design give each of these cutouts a designed feel, while exterior mounted artifacts leave no space lacking character.

A simple adobe structure, topped with thatching, provides simple accommodation for tools and equipment at the agricultural center. Keeping it local, and keeping it real, keeps Loreto Bay charming.

Doors exhibit historic craftsmanship along with a sense of
security and privacy.

Adobe is a wonderful, organic medium for construction. The walls enter the home as furnishings, too, with fireplace hearths, window ledges, and built-in benches becoming extensions of the builder's imagination.

Studded metal chairs and a wrought-iron lighting fixture embody the Spanish influence on Mexican sensibilities.

Furnishings exemplary of fine craftsmanship find themselves at home in a sculpted adobe structure. Here a raised ceiling and paned windows expand the feeling of space in an intimate dining room.

Wood furnishings express Spanish colonial aesthetics, at home amidst terracotta and the exposed beams of a stucco home.

A great room incorporates kitchen, dining, and lounge areas in keeping with today's growing tradition toward connectedness and away from more formal traditions.

A spacious kitchen embodies the wood, stucco, and tile craftsmanship traditional to the region, while incorporating the modern appliances and conveniences sought by today's connoisseurs.

A window opens over a serving counter, connecting kitchen with dining area.

Wooden beams reveal the home's natural structure, allowing architecture to be a dominant part of the décor.

Terracotta floors underline a room finished in stark white outline, and furnished with warm woods and leathers.

Blue is a wonderful accent color that has found its way into the homes of many of the early Loreto Bay colonists. The rich cobalt hue evokes sea and sky at their zenith.

Glass connects the living areas with the inner courtyard for a sense that one is never far from what's important.

Terracotta tones serve as palette for furnishings of chocolate and cream.

A grand, open floorplan provides a wonderful setting where family members can find their favorite corner to curl up in, or at times, fill the space with friends.

Inside rooms and exterior are inextricably connected in the Spanish courtyard culture. A vaulted brick ceiling recalls classic architecture and craftsmanship.

Werner Segarra Photography

Photo by Russ Heinl

A close-up explores the detail of an artisan-crafted, vaulted brick ceiling.

Werner Segarra Photography

Indoor living spaces are never far from a source of natural light. Mexican inspired design is beautifully married with light efficiency in a living room where the walls slide back to admit fresh air.

Two views explored the staggered brick ceiling alcove that vents a kitchen area.

Loggia are the covered walkways that partially or fully encircle the central courtyard in traditional Spanish architecture. Arched doorways provide broad access to the garden area and, usually, a fountain.

Two views of a first and second-floor loggia are viewed from the central courtyard of a hotel in the old city of Loreto.

A loggia area can be enclosed or opened via folding doors.

A terrace on the second floor is connected with the rooms on the main floor via a courtyard. In clement weather like that afforded by Mexico, these courtyard doors will often stand open, allowing air to circulate freely through the home.

Spain brought a "courtyard culture" to the New World, and folks living in the Southwest have reveled in it ever since. New homes in The Village incorporate the best to be found in this domestic feature: outdoor *cocinas*, *piscinas*, and *fuentes* or kitchens, pools, and fountains.

Curving walls, one tiled in terra-cotta-toned tiles, and a three-tiered fountain characterize a meandering courtyard rich in color, texture, and appeal.

A spacious custom home in the new Villages development opens
to an inviting courtyard complete with pristine pool.

Tiered fountains are signature touches in Loreto Bay courtyards.

A community courtyard in the villages creates
a park-like center where people can mingle.

It's all about detail in this lower-level courtyard. A rustic red tile floor ties together natural wood door and window frames, cream stucco walls, and wall art chosen by the homeowner. Tropical plants surround a peaceful fountain centerpiece, while a unique window connects the private space to the street.

Economy of space didn't limit the owner from incorporating a personal spa in their private courtyard.

Retirement or resort living almost dictates that lounging, eating, cooking, and socializing take place next to sparking water and a profusion of tropical plants.

Photo by Russ Heinl

Photo by Russ Heinl

A ceiling fan circulates air, kept cool by thick adobe walls.

Traditional mission-style furniture is fitting accompaniment to stucco walls.

A room in the Inn at Loreto Bay celebrates the colors of sunshine, Mexican style.

Palm motifs keep the focus on the "escape" aspect of establishing a home in Baja, Mexico.

Four examples on whirlpool tub installations in new homes within the village.

Photo by Russ Heinl

79

Vanities in the washrooms feature locally manufactured tile and porcelain sinks.

His and hers kayaks wait, poised to take their owners on the ever-unfolding adventure that is the Sea of Cortez.

The Villages' master plan for phase one of the development dictates close ties to the water. Backyards will function like estuaries and the Sea of Cortez is always just a short walk away. Many of these soft-edged estuaries and more structured canals will commence their five-mile, meandering journey through Loreto Bay in Agua Viva. These waterways will offer delightful kayaking opportunities (in many cases, right from your home!), and will provide a refuge and/or nursery for an array of marine life and waterfowl adding to the kayak experience.

Walls of woven palm and a thatched roof express native ingenuity and resourcefulness at a kayak rental station on the beach.

Survival of Tradition

Although the vision for a sustainable community in Loreto is new, the city boasts a long and proud history upon which to build.

The first Catholic missionary from Spain visited the region in 1697 and began working with the then primitive Native population. Soon after, cattle were introduced, agriculture was developed, and the locals were put to work creating thread and knitting wool under the auspices of the mission. The Mission San Javier is found a few miles south of Loreto, begun in 1744 and finished in 1759.

The city served as capital to the Baja region during 133 years of Spanish colonial rule. It was also the launching point for Father Junipero Serra's historic trek northward to establish the now-famous California missions.

The Sierra La Giganta mountains that tower to the west of the town are a wonderland for birders. Native trees and plants green the hills with subtle beauty, and offer a smorgasbord of herbs and edibles for the wild crafter.

In the sea, five deserted islands seem to float on the horizon, and serve as home to pelicans and lion seals.

The Mexican government targeted Loreto for economic development in the 1970s, pouring development funds and promotion into the site. However, the resort languished with the exception of those who came for its nearly legendary sport fishing, including teeming populations of yellowtail, marlin, sailfish, and dorado.

The sun sets on The Mission San Javier, which can be found a few miles south of Loreto, built in 1744 and finished in 1759.

Photo by Russ Heinl

Catholicism came to the Baja peninsula in 1697 with the first Spanish missionary, Jesuit Juan María de Salvatierra. He established Mission Loreto on October 25th, a successful enterprise that is considered the mother of the subsequent missions that spread up the coast of California.

Inside Mission San Javier a local museum traces the history of the city: a must see for any visitor to the city. Loreto Bay Company hires cabs and drops potential buyers off before its doors to ensure that would-be residents have this opportunity.

A distinctive feature of downtown Loreto, the arched trees lend charm and shade to this historic cobblestone thoroughfare.

Local pride makes for picture perfect views of Mexicana. Local gift shops sell the pottery, porcelain, silver, mother-of-pearl, and other indigenous treasures snapped up by tourists.

A Belief in the Future

The Three Pillars

The most commonly understood aspect of sustainability is respecting and preserving the environment, but there are actually three areas of sustainable development the company refers to as "The Three Pillars."

1. Environmental Sustainability: Preserving and enhancing the ecosystem locally and globally by measuring and improving our impact on the environment.

2. Social Sustainability: Improving the health and welfare of a community and region; providing opportunities for local jobs and business creation; personal growth, education, health, and lifelong learning.

3. Economic Sustainability: Profit due to sound business practices: measurable cost benefits from strategic sustainability policies, such as conservation of water and energy; creating wealth for investors and homeowners; jobs for people in the community; and new business development in the local economy.

Photo by Russ Heinl

WELCOME TO
LORETO BAY ECOSCAPES
AGRICULTURAL CENTER

GARBAGE
BASURA

With production, efficiency, and a 100-percent organic approach, the Ecoscapes agricultural center cultivates native wildlife for integration in Loreto Bay's communities and gardens. It also provides jobs for local residents, supporting both the environmental and economic initiatives of the Loreto Bay Foundation. An organic farm to produce fresh food just minutes from the new homes is up and running.

By creating jobs that support the mission of the Loreto Bay Company, residents can participate in a global economy without sacrificing their values.

Several acres of an experimental site have been set aside for cultivating ornamental plants. The goal is to work with plants that can tolerate briny water, a resource more widely available and less costly to the environment than the fresh water reserved for potable uses in the nearby mountain aquifer.

Construction and homebuilding are inherently invasive to an environment. However, the Loreto Bay Foundation has gone to great pains to preserve as much native vegetation as possible. Tress are transplanted rather than bulldozed. In the case of these native trees, scientists discovered that a multi-step process was imperative to save them. The walls of these transportation boxes were actually put around the tree while it was still in its original space. After auxiliary roots were allowed to heal from the initial invasion, the bottom taproot can then be severed and the tree removed. The alternative, of course, is a dead tree and the many years required to start over from seed.

Shade-loving plants at the Loreto Bay Ecoscapes Agricultural Center are cultivated for private courtyards and public areas.

Making it Happen

Q. How can we make human settlement positive for the environment?

Produce more energy from renewable resources than we consume;
Harvest or produce more water than we use;
Create more biodiversity, biomass, and habitat than existed when we started.

Seals are a tourist draw in Loreto, with chartered boats promising sightings.

Pelicans play the crystal waters and encircle the skies around the Villages of Loreto Bay. If the developers do their job as intended, there will be more of these majestic birds, not less.

Q. How can we improve social welfare?

Establish a foundation and dedicate one percent of the gross proceeds of all sales and resales, in perpetuity to assist with local social and community issues. So far, nearly one million dollars has been donated to the Foundation by Loreto Bay Company, with over three million dollars pledged.

Implement a Regional Affordable Housing Strategy to ensure that people who work at Loreto Bay are able to afford to live in the area.

Support the development of a full service medical center in Loreto.

Establish a foundation

The Loreto Bay Foundation was established to support and fund local projects in the community of Loreto, Baja California Sur, and in the Loreto Bay National Marine Park. The project must be "organized and operated for charitable purposes" (i.e., not a for-profit venture). Project staff are allowed to earn a fair salary for their work on the project, but investors are not allowed to make a profit from the project. The principal benefactors of LBF are the Loreto Bay Company and the residents of Loreto Bay.

In 2005, time was spent talking to people in the town of Loreto to research quality of life issues and existing infrastructure. Key community leaders, especially non-profit representatives, were interviewed as part of a research project to identify potential grantees to be inaugural recipients at the official launch of LBF. As of April, $2 million had been dedicated to the Foundation, and regular disbursements were underway toward the establishment of a better community.

Eleven charities affiliated with Loreto have received inaugural grants that total $64,350 to assist them in their efforts toward creating a better community. Among these was an animal welfare grant to Animalandia, a spaying and neutering project, which will help in the construction of their new facility. An environment grant was awarded to Grupo Ecologista Antares, A.C., for the building of a new environmental center. The Loreto campus of the state university (UABCS), the Loreto Fire Department, and the Center of Ecotourism and Sustainable Development at Stanford University, are among others that have been awarded funds.

A special fund was created to benefit the children of Loreto. It focuses on improving their quality of life. A primary activity of this fund will be to support the annual Christmas Present Project. Every year, the Loreto chapter of Cáritas (an international charity) sponsors a Christmas present project. A tree is placed in the courtyard of the Loreto Mission, and Loretanos are asked to donate wrapped presents to be distributed to the less fortunate children of Loreto. The presents are marked with appropriate age and gender, and Cáritas volunteers drive through various lower-income neighborhoods and distribute them. The present distribution takes place over a few days around Christmas and covers the Loreto neighborhoods of Miramar and Zaragoza (as well as surrounding villages, including San Bruno, San Javier, and Ensenada Blanca). In addition, Cáritas volunteers prepare and deliver Christmas dinners, blankets, and children's presents to a pre-selected list of families in need.

When LBC staff member, Siri Thomas, discovered the Christmas tree three years ago, she offered to accept financial donations from friends and family to purchase and wrap presents. With the help of some generous donors, she was able to contribute a few hundred presents. In 2004, with the help of financial contributions from Team Loreto Bay (and lots of wrapping help from Loreto Bay Company employees), LBC and Siri contributed approximately 600 presents and also sponsored six families with dinners, blankets, and presents!

The Loreto Bay Foundation (through its US "host" Foundation, The Ocean Foundation) accepted and tracked donations earmarked for the Loreto Christmas Present Project. As a result, donations to the Loreto Children Fund became tax-deductible. Through this new mechanism, Siri's friends and family as well as Team Loreto Bay contributed $6,939. This translated into 600 presents (each individually wrapped!), 66 blankets, and 41 meals for children and families in Loreto.

The creation of the Loreto Children Fund as a vehicle for this project insures that any excess funds (beyond what is needed for the Christmas Present Project) will be earmarked specifically for the benefit of the children of Loreto.

Photo by Russ Heinl

Implement a Regional Affordable Housing Strategy

Loreto Bay is working with Federal, State, and local governments, international agencies, and Mexican contractors to develop an integrated program that will leverage a variety of resources to ensure a sustainable social housing program for the greater region of Loreto. Infonavit, the Mexican Government's social housing agency, and the largest developer/sponsor of housing in the world, is actively engaged. For those workers without sufficient credits to participate in the Infonavit citizen's mortgage plan, alternative solutions, such as rent-to-own, are being explored.

A deep respect for the local culture is an integral part of the Loreto Bay development, as is the integration of Mexicans and non-Mexicans in making this a successful sustainable community. The current population of Loreto is 12,000, and is expected to more than double to 25,000 or more in the next five to ten years. Loreto Bay Company is committed to paying a generous living wage for workers and has required all sub-contractors to pay wages above industry norms for this area. By doing so, the company hopes to make the dream of homeownership a reality for many citizens of Loreto.

One of the first impacts of a large real estate development project is often a huge influx of construction workers. The Mexican Constitution requires all companies to provide "adequate housing" for their employees. Employers are also required to pay a percentage of a worker's salary to the National Worker's Housing Development Fund Institute (Infonavit) to implement housing programs for workers, or finance the construction or improvement of workers' dwellings.

The Loreto Bay Foundation, as part of its mission, has helped mitigate the impacts of this development project on the community of Loreto. LBF has assisted in supporting architectural plans for worker housing, advising the Loreto Bay Company on measures to remind contractors and labor brokers of their legal obligations, and performed routine spot checks of worker housing standards compliance, among others.

Further enhancements of a worker's quality of life include education and alternative entertainment when they are off duty. To address this issue, the Loreto Workers Fund will assist in the development of projects such as: a small library with books and games, opportunities to obtain a GED equivalent, and ESL classes.

FONATUR Photography

Support the development of a full service medical center in Loreto

Health care in Loreto is currently sub-standard, and serious improvements are required. The Loreto Bay Foundation has created a special fund that focuses on the improvement of the medical services for the inhabitants of Loreto by supporting the creation of a state-of-the-art medical facility. The construction of the Loreto hospital is expected to be completed by the end of the summer (2007) and operational by the end of 2007. The hospital will provide outpatient and inpatient services treating adult and pediatric medical conditions. It will also have one surgical operating room and one labor and delivery suite.

The relative isolation of Loreto has provided a difficult challenge for the provision of quality health care for its residents. This has been evidenced by the inability to recruit specialty physicians as well as by the lack of modern, sophisticated medical equipment. Currently, the level of medicine is that of a rural general practice. Eighteen family physicians practice in three different general practice clinics. The hospital, the Centro de Salud, is essentially a clinic with basic laboratory and imaging capability. There is no operating theatre or ICU. There is no blood bank, ultrasound, or CT scanner. Patients who require admission are stabilized then transferred by ground to the regional hospital in Constitucion, a journey of one hundred and twenty kilometers or two-and-a-half hours away. The major referral hospital for the State is in La Paz, another hour and a half south of Constitucion. Trauma care is a significant problem for residents and tourists. Loreto is situated on the trans-peninsular highway and vehicular traumas, as well as sport related accidents, are frequent. Delays in treatment for trauma, cardiac emergencies, and complications of pregnancy have resulted in increased morbidity and mortality for the patients. The need for improvements in the quality of medical care is immediate.

Q. How can we ensure economic growth?

Create significant new jobs in Loreto.
Enhance the local economy through responsible tourism and new business development.
Build a successful community that delivers a healthy rate of return to our investors, homeowners, and partners.

The Inn at Loreto Bay provides employment to local citizens. The inn's role as hub and host site for potential customers to the new village's development has boosted sagging tourism to the area.

Photo by Russ Heinl

About the Loreto Bay Company

Loreto Bay Company is committed to a philosophy of treading lightly, and to making Loreto Bay a sustainable community. This includes environmental preservation, creating jobs, and devoting a portion of home sales to the community and setting aside 5,000 acres as a natural preserve. Being a sustainable community also means harvesting more potable water than the new residents consume in order to enhance the existing natural streams and marshes and nurture the biodiversity of the land The Villages occupies.

Werner Segarra Photography